# FASHION CATS
## Unchained
## Coloring Book

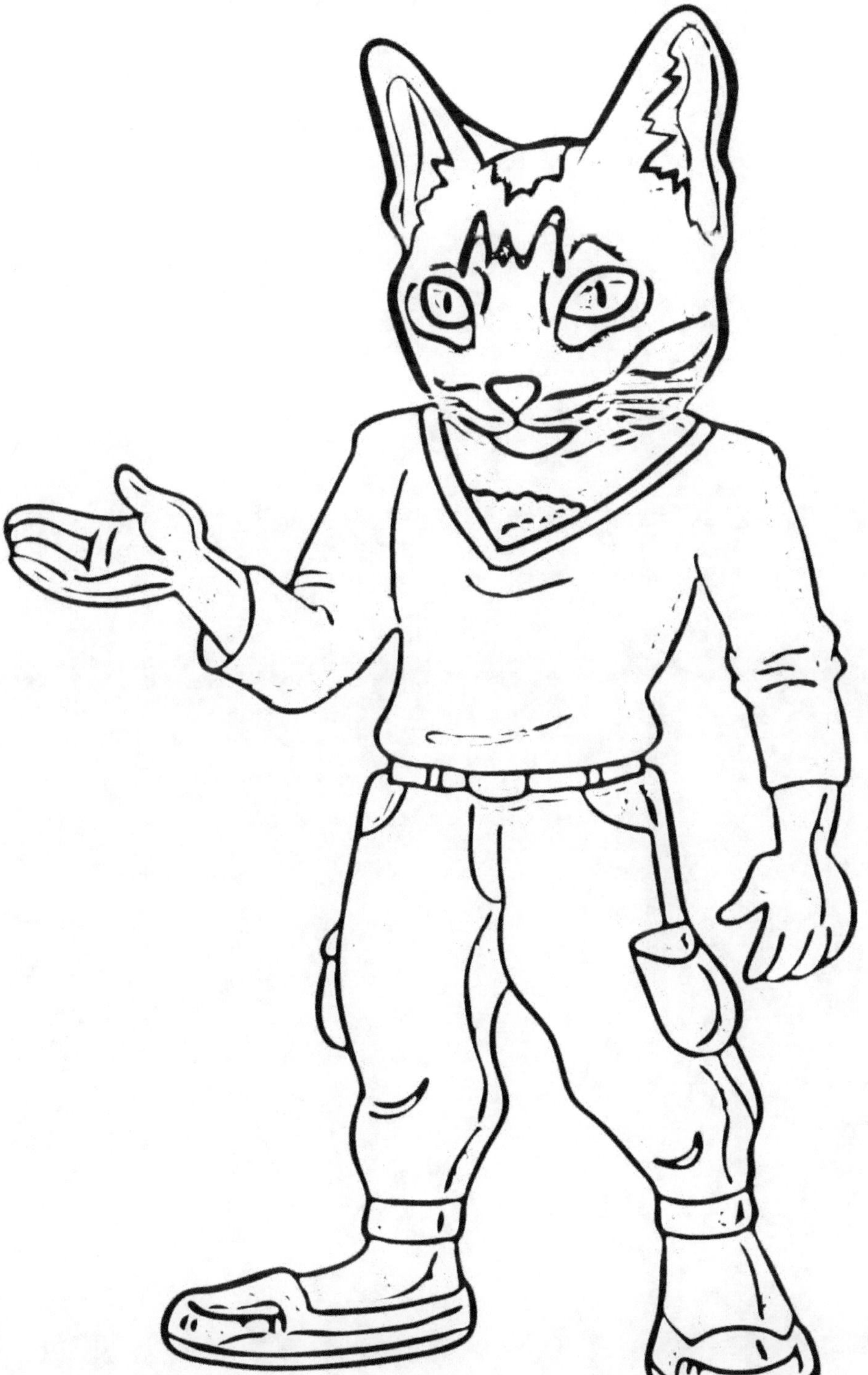

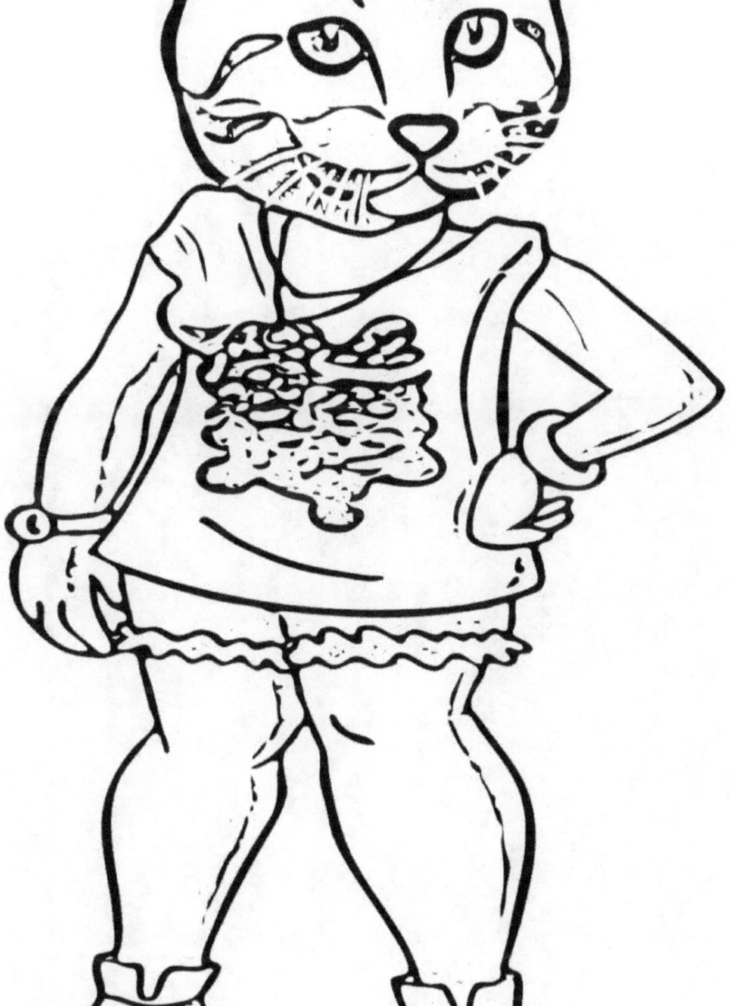

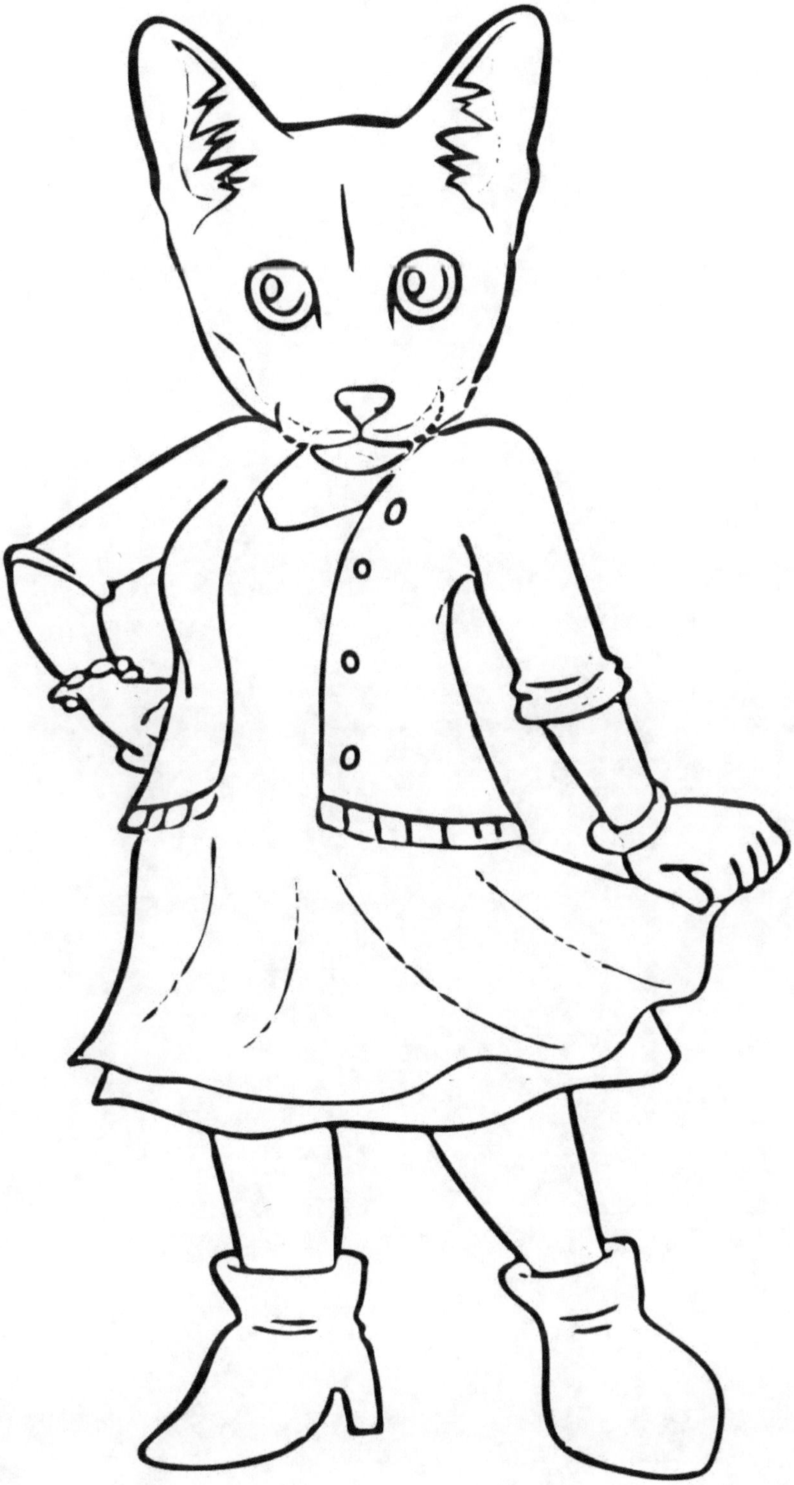

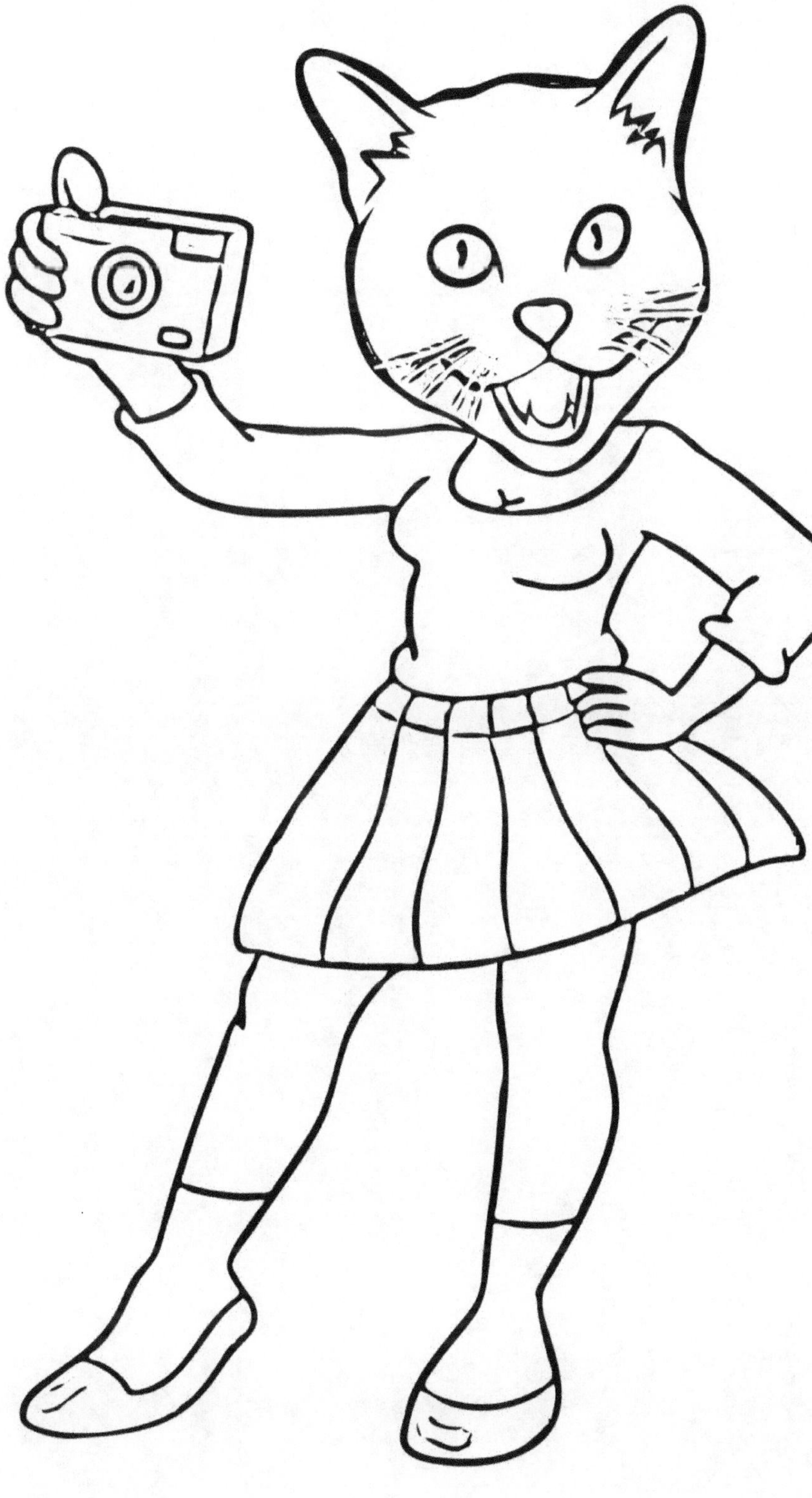

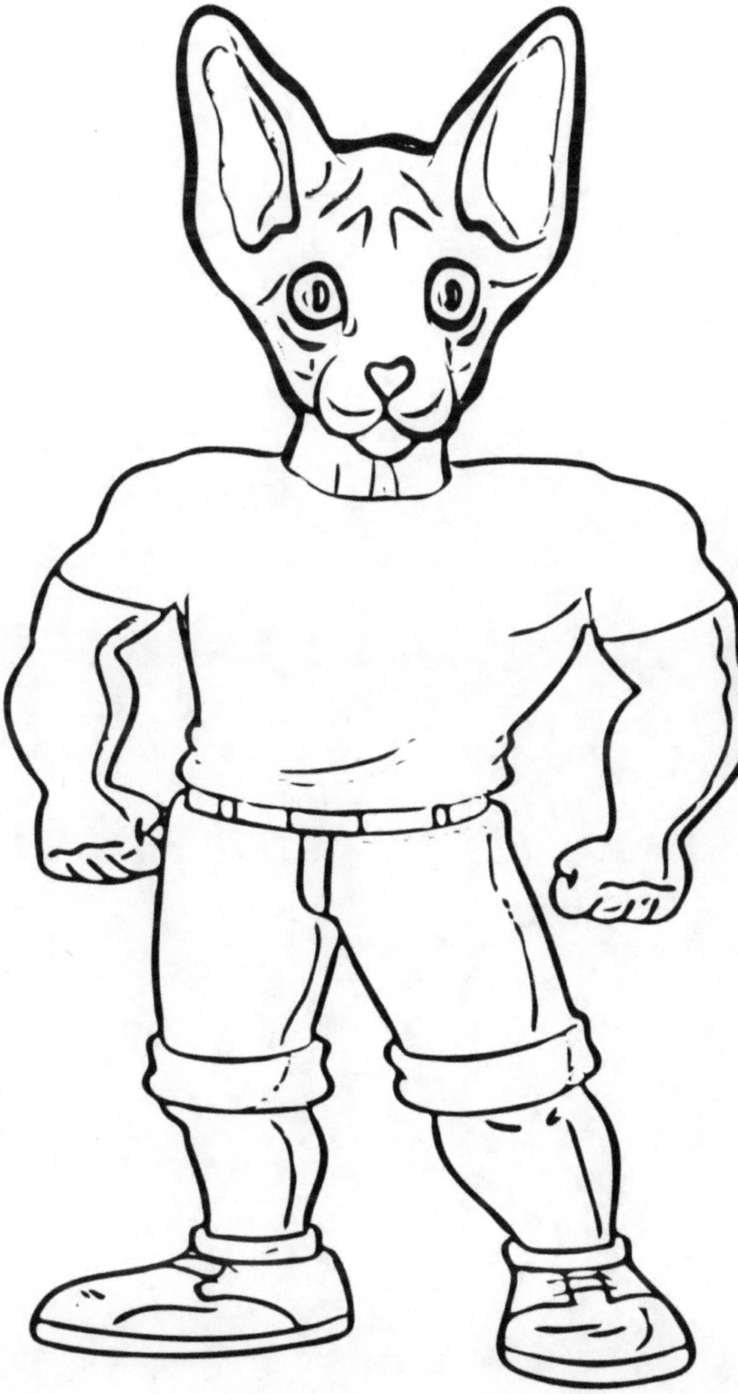

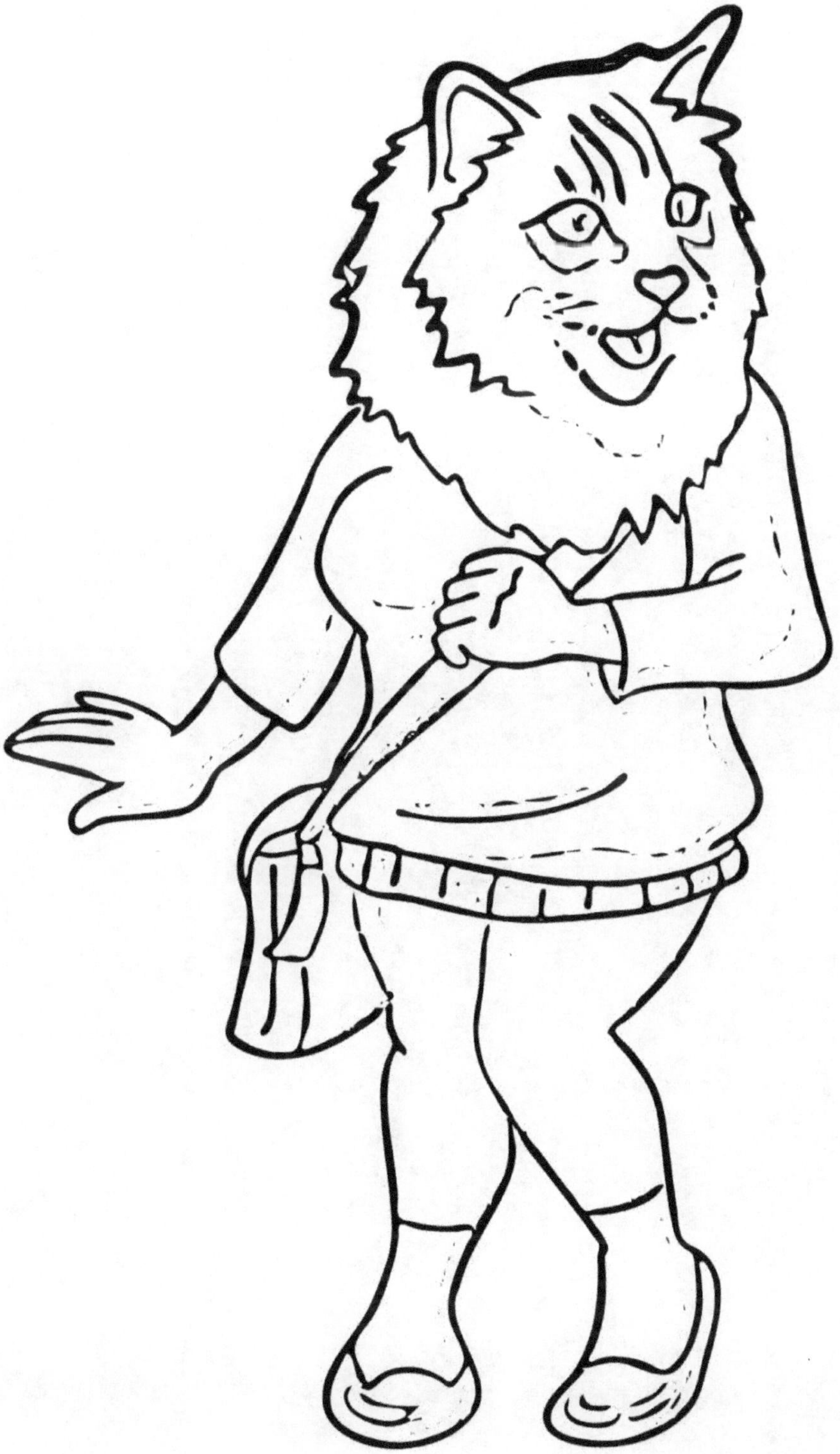

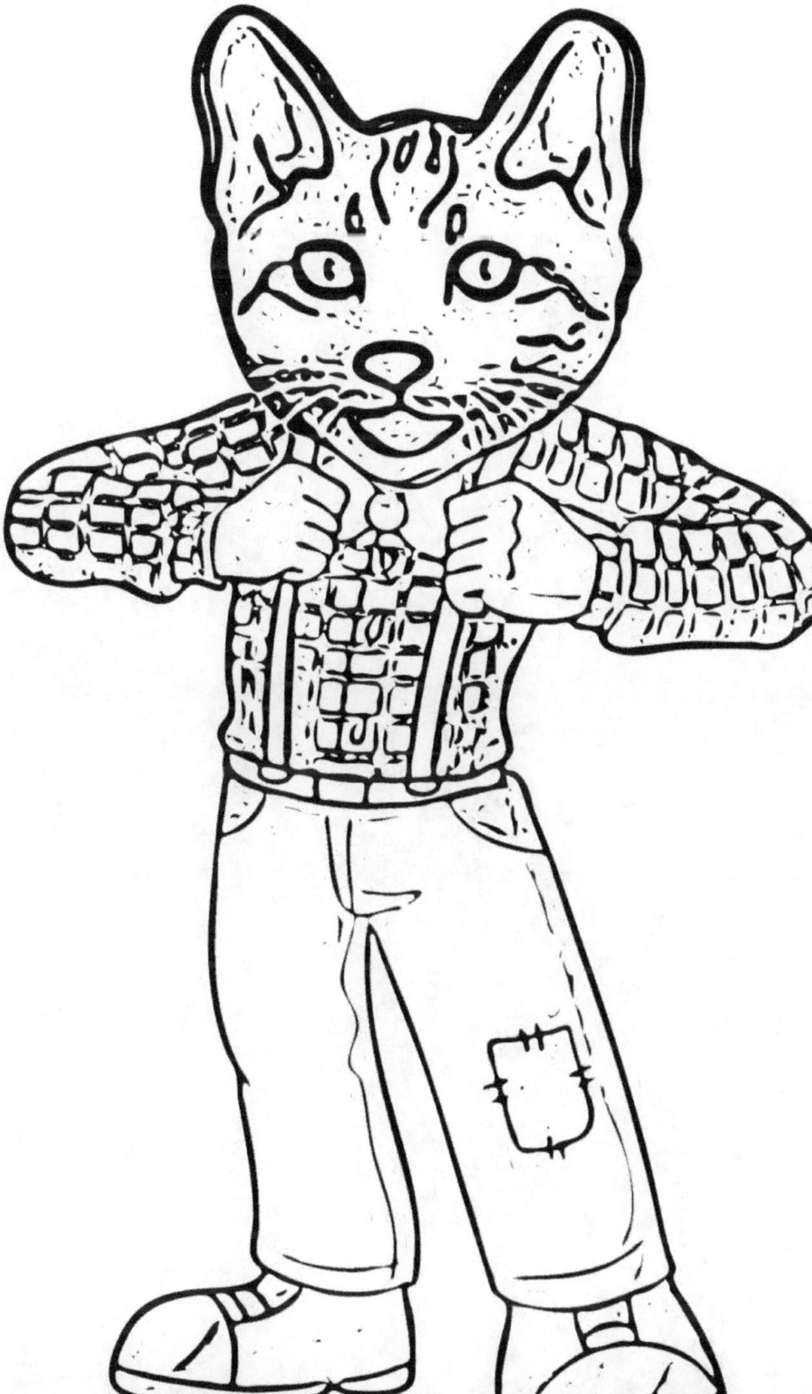

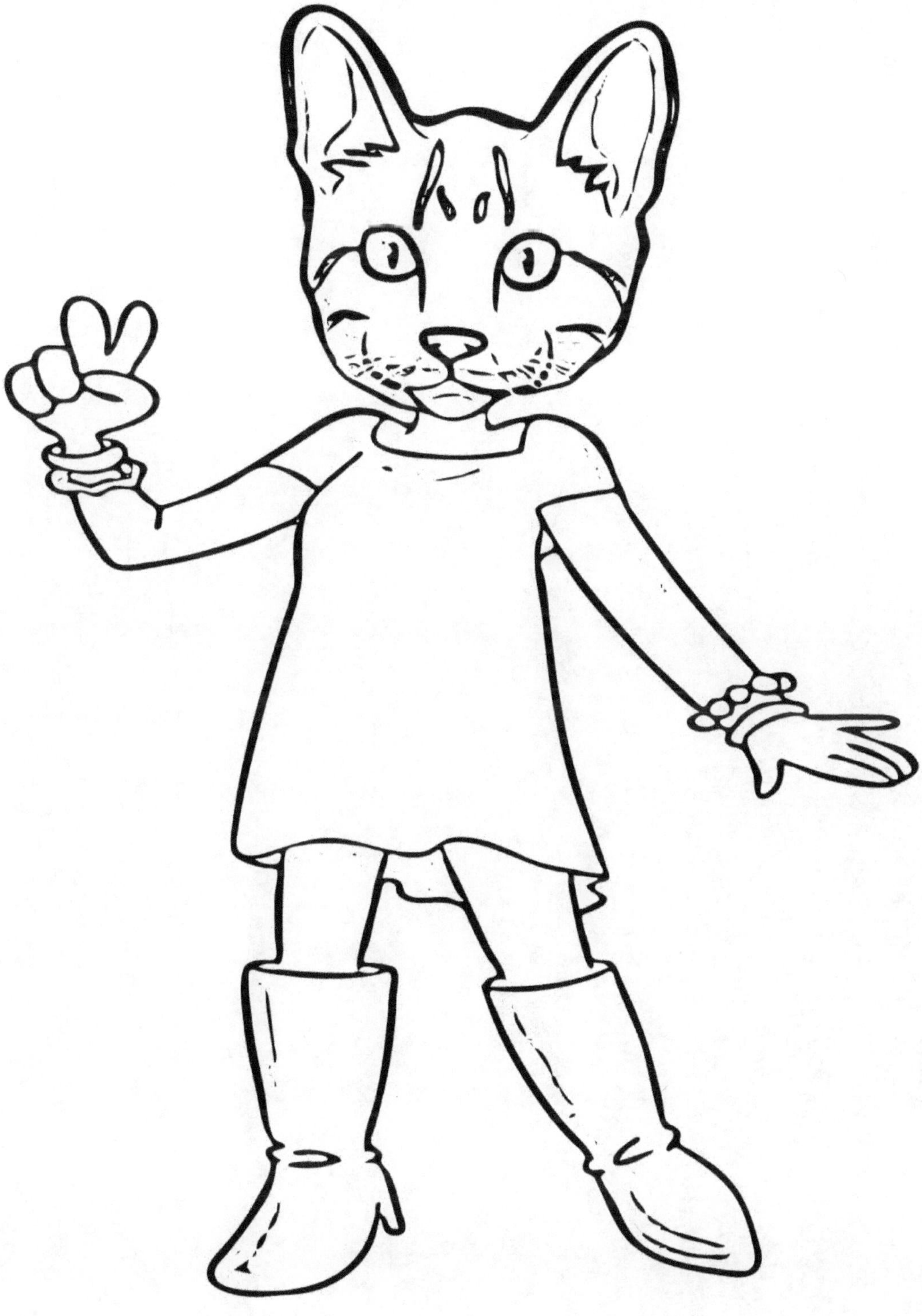

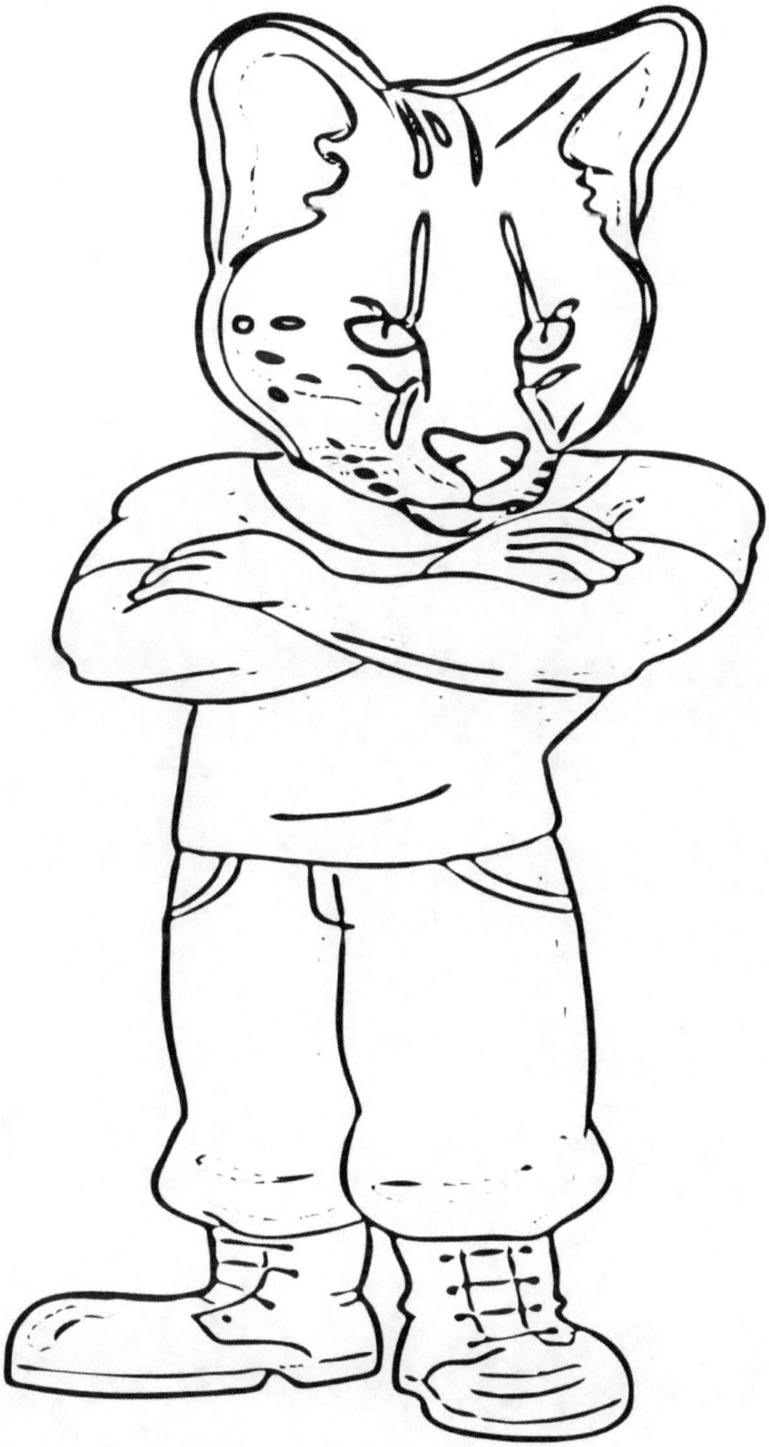

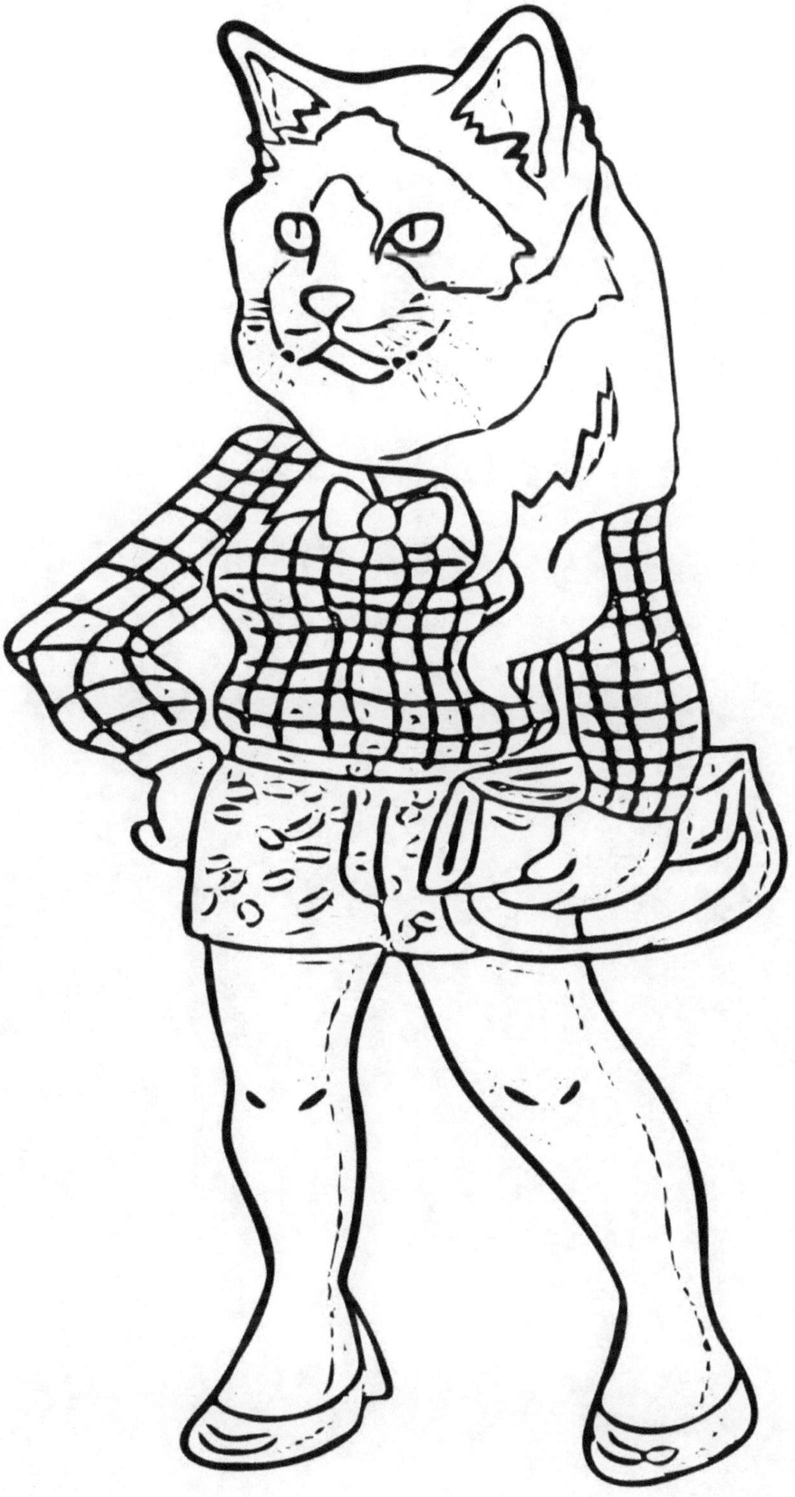

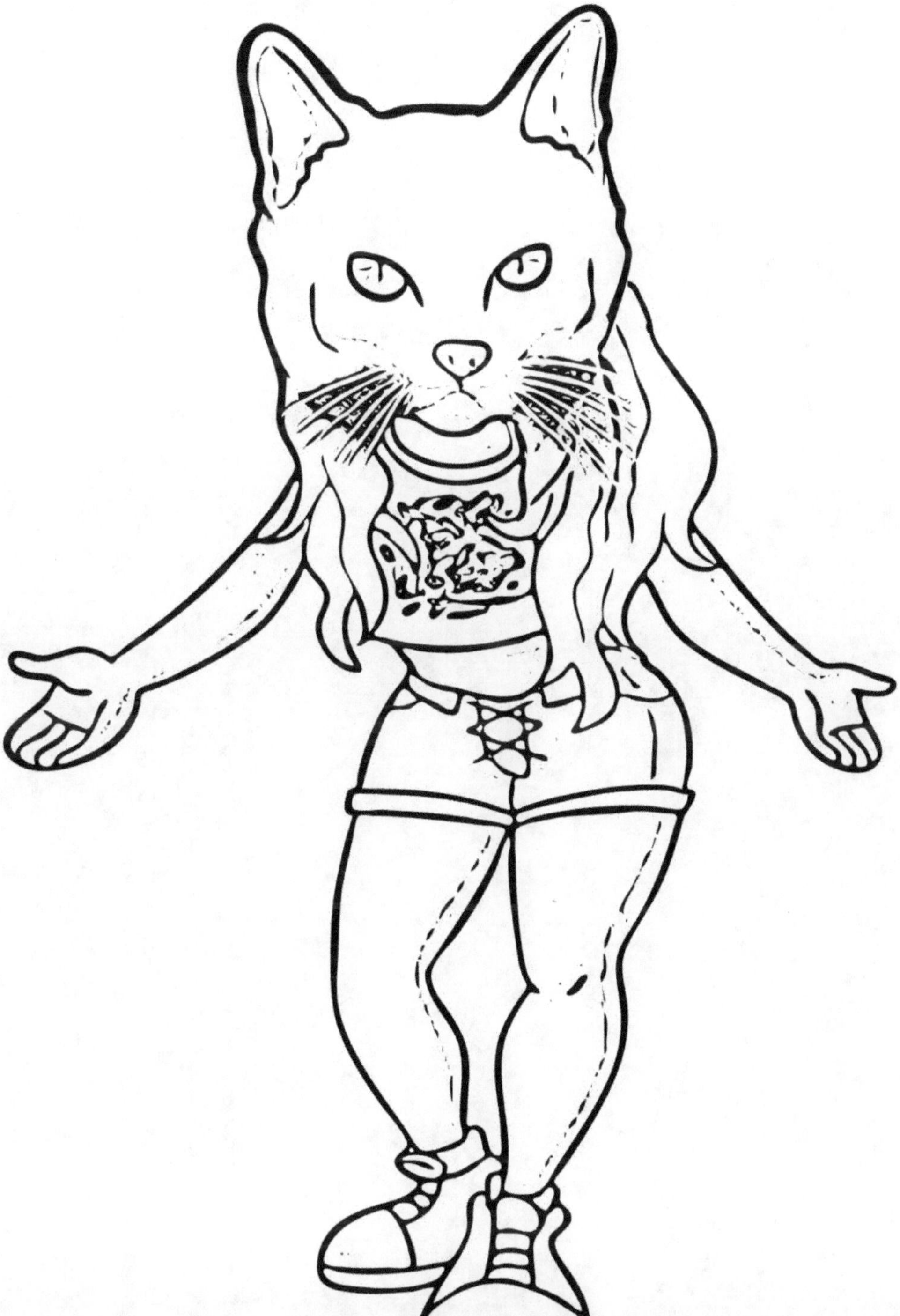

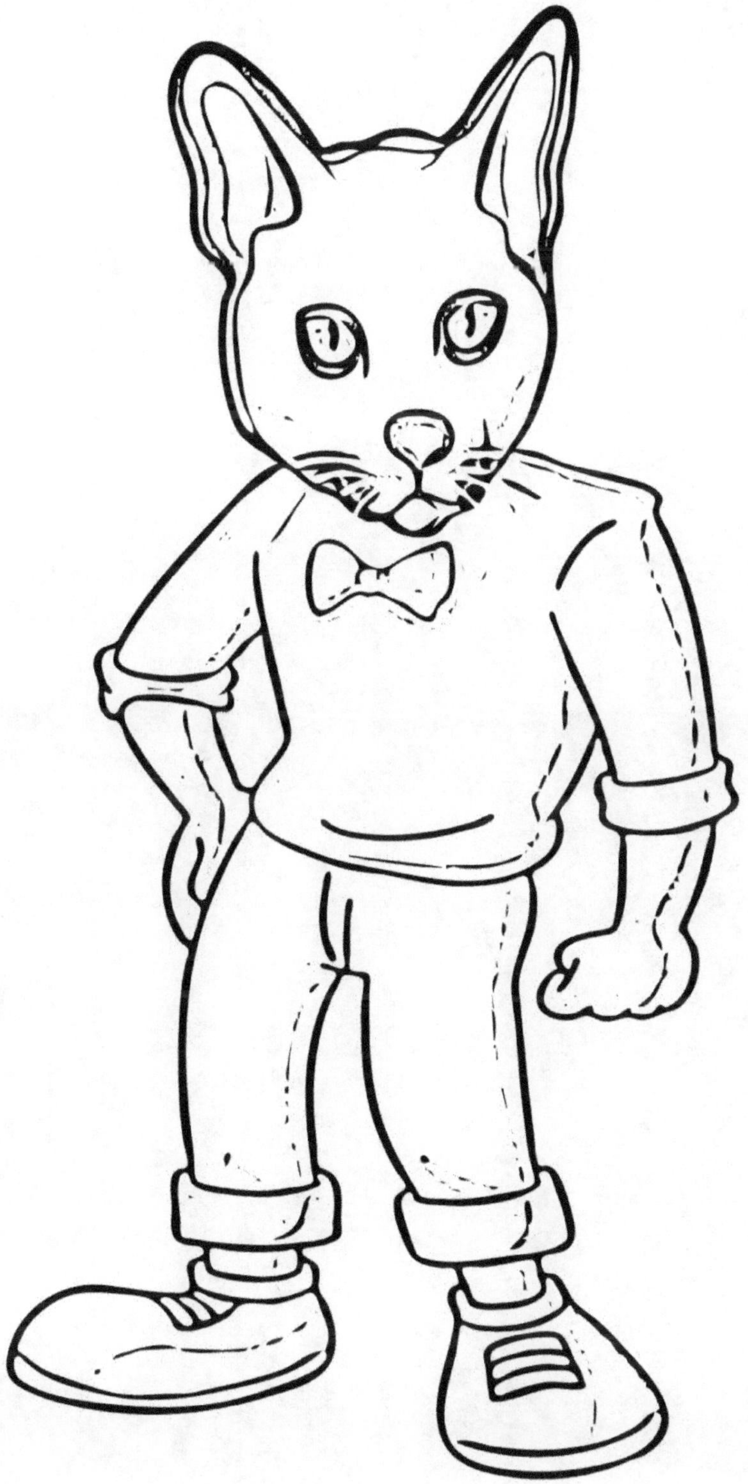

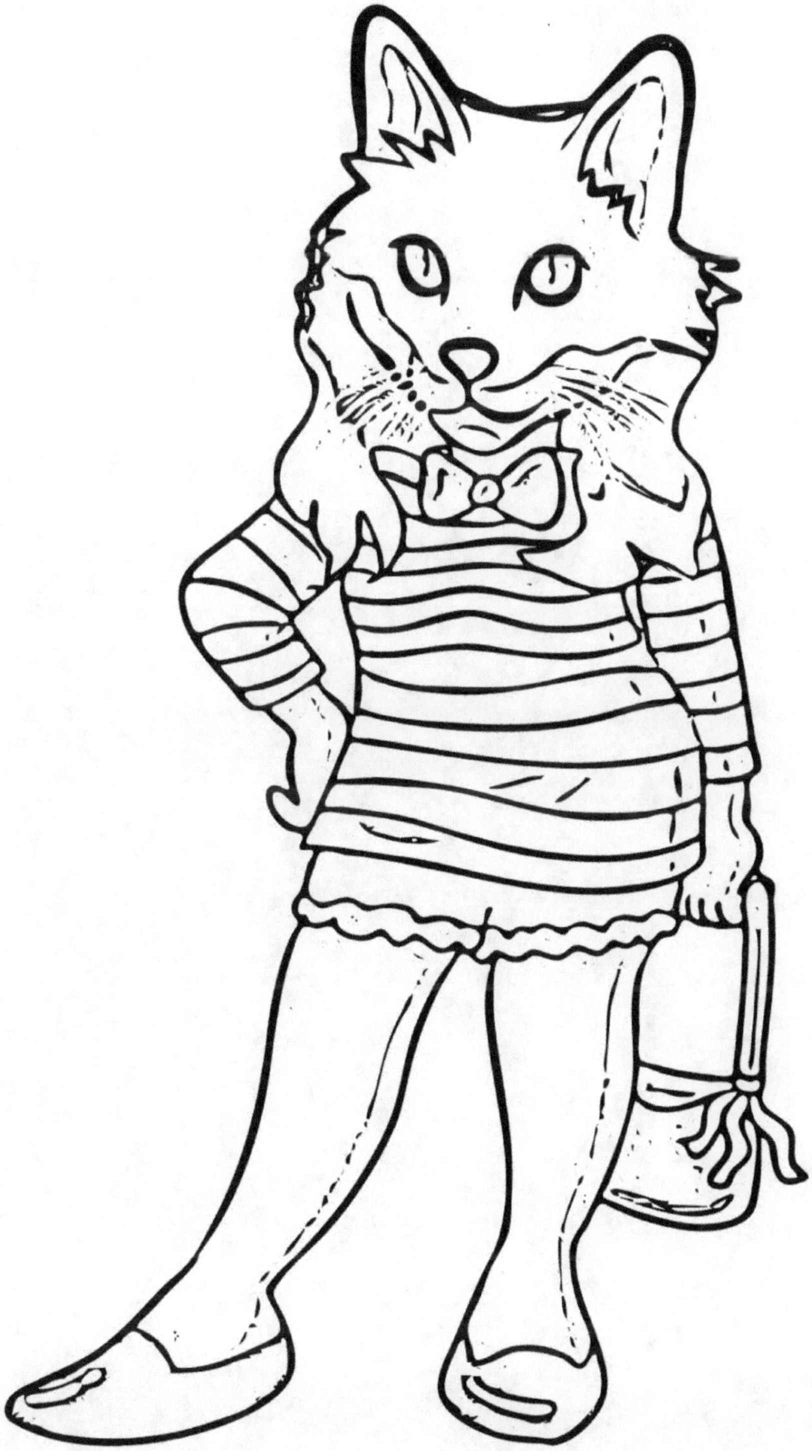

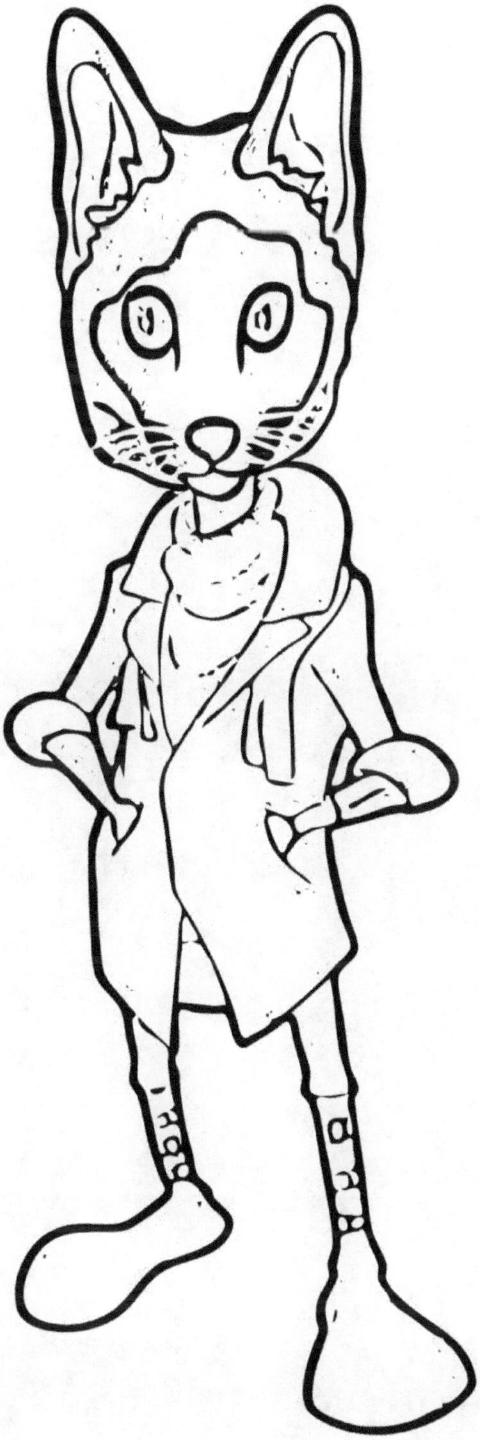

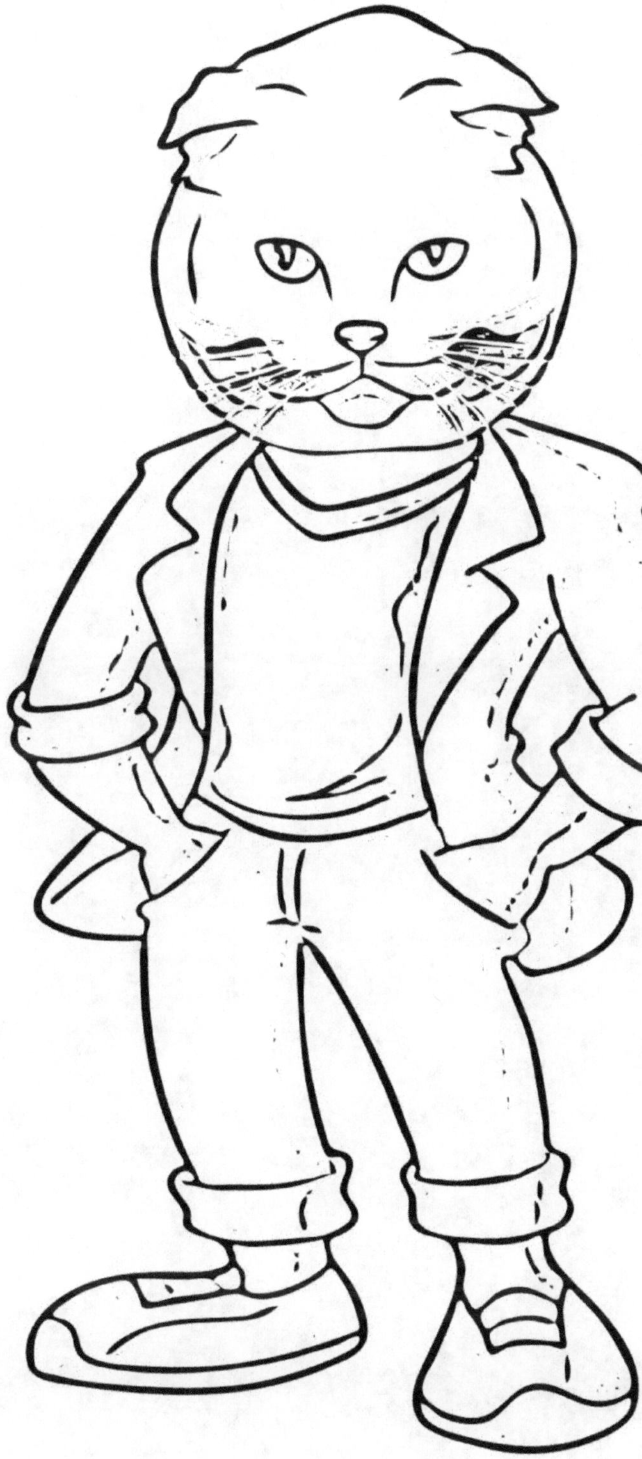

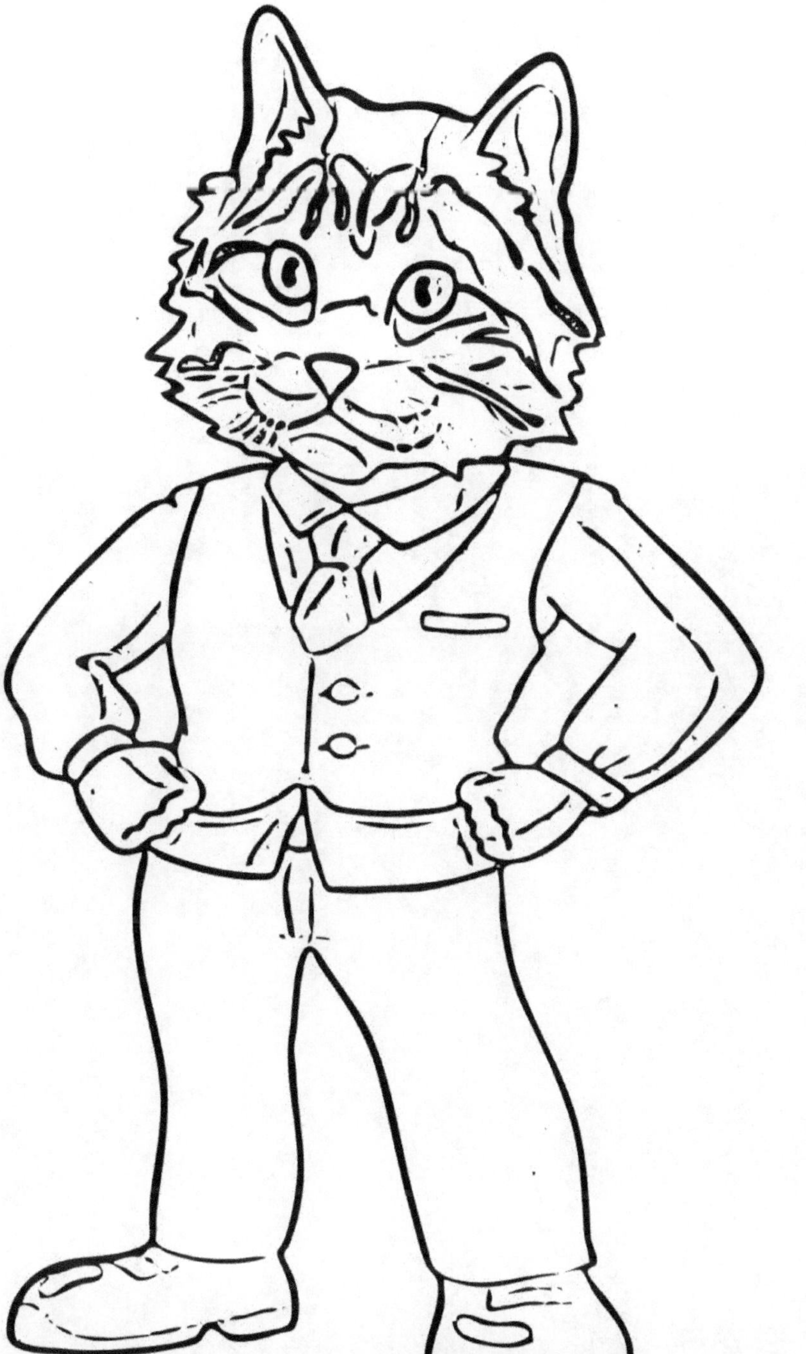

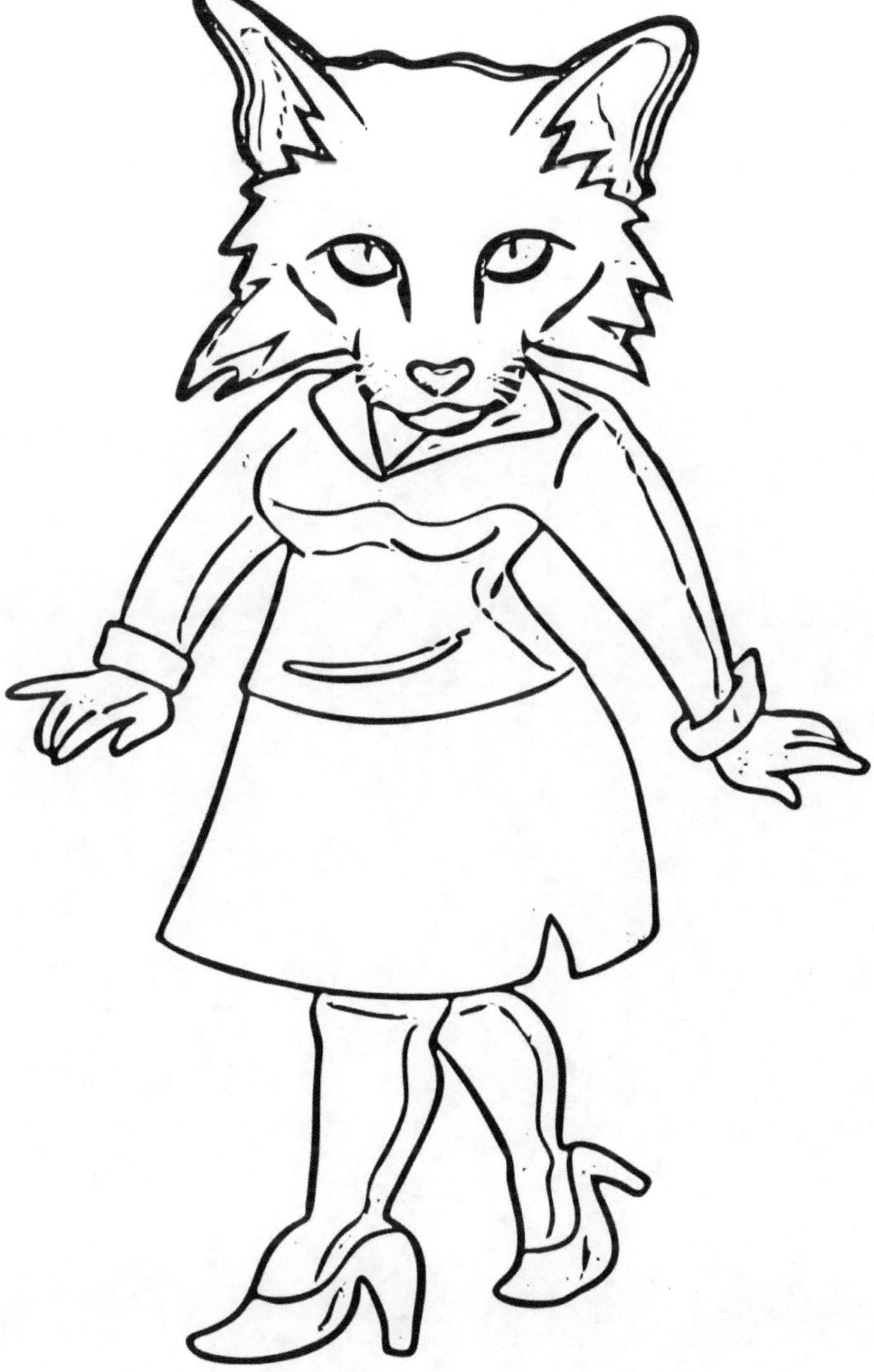

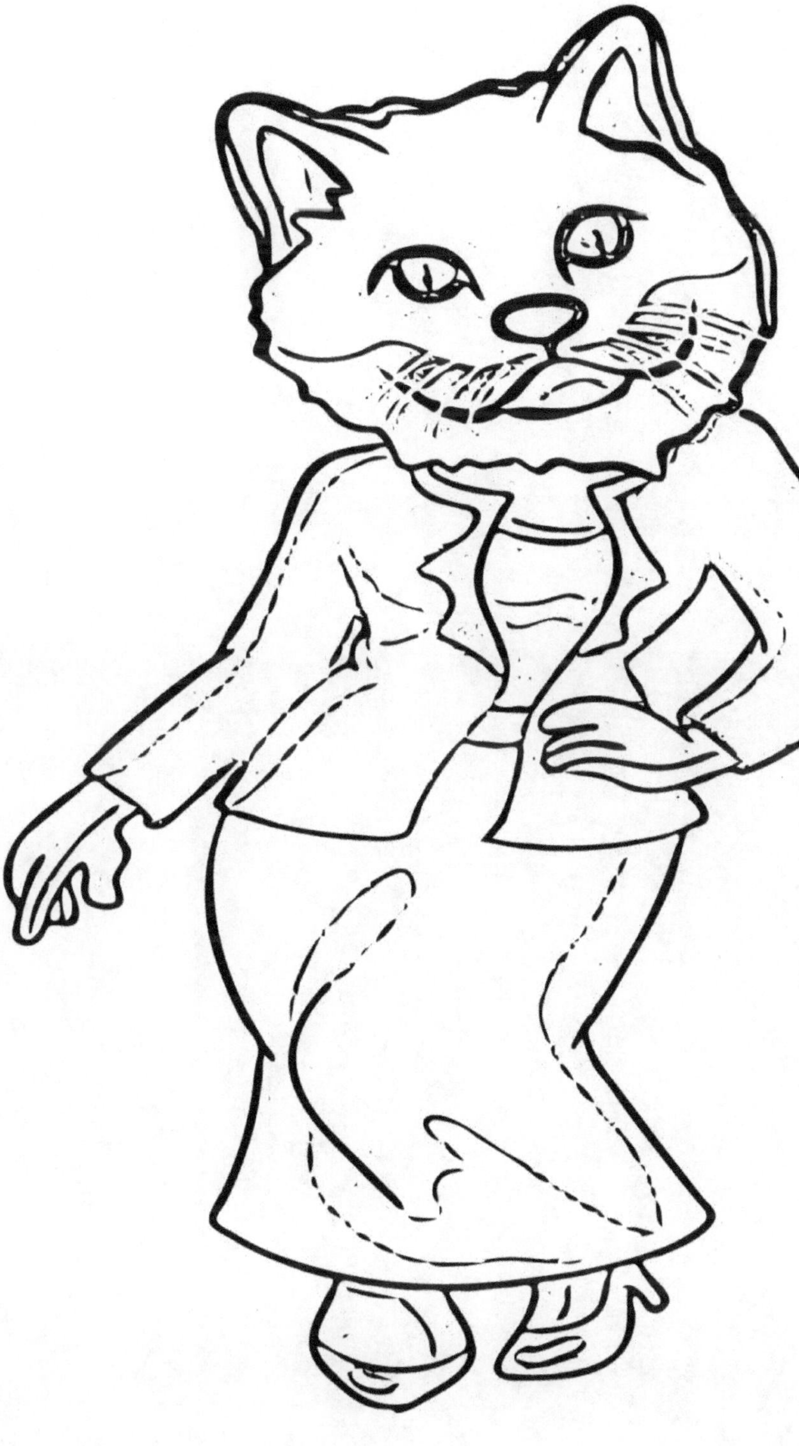

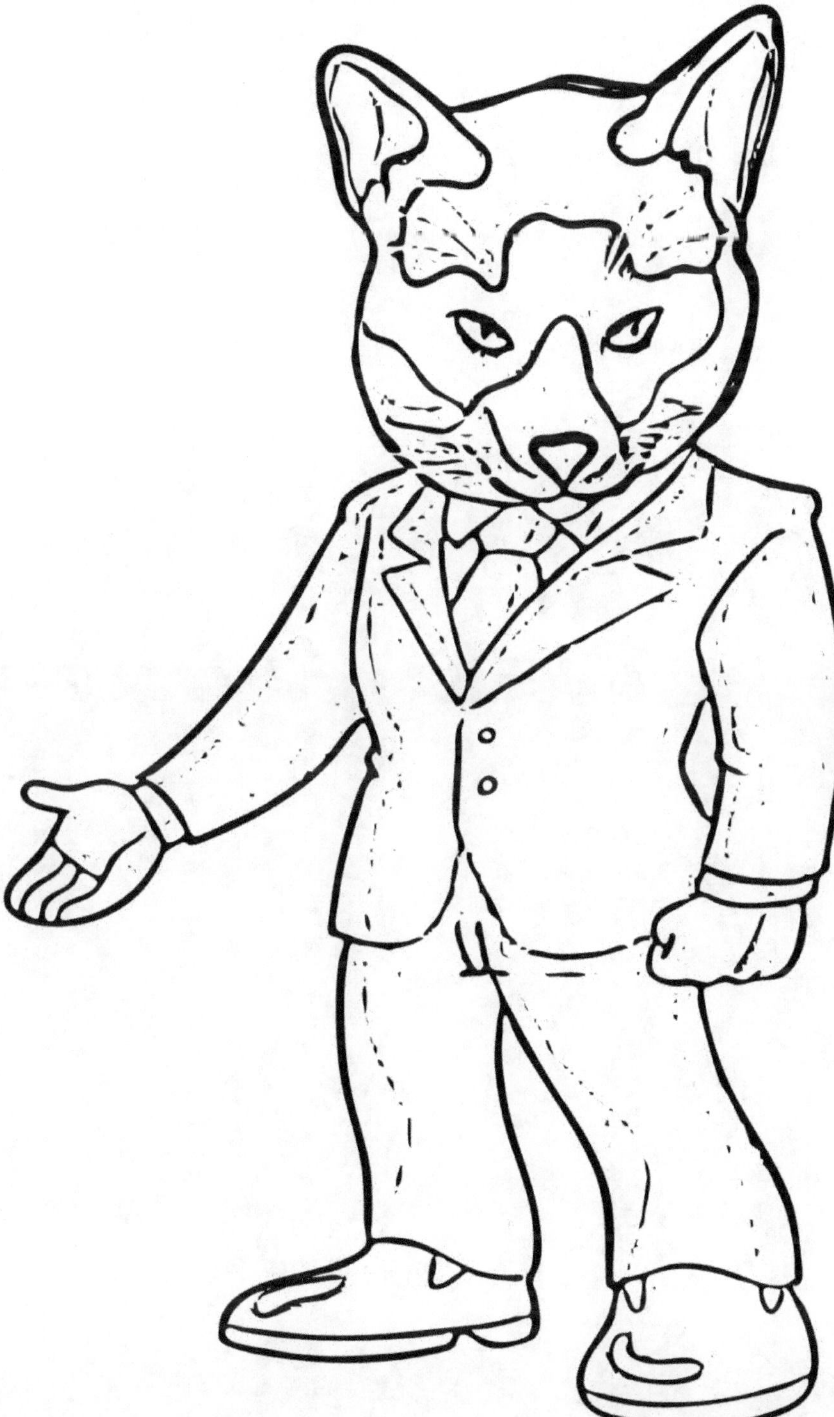

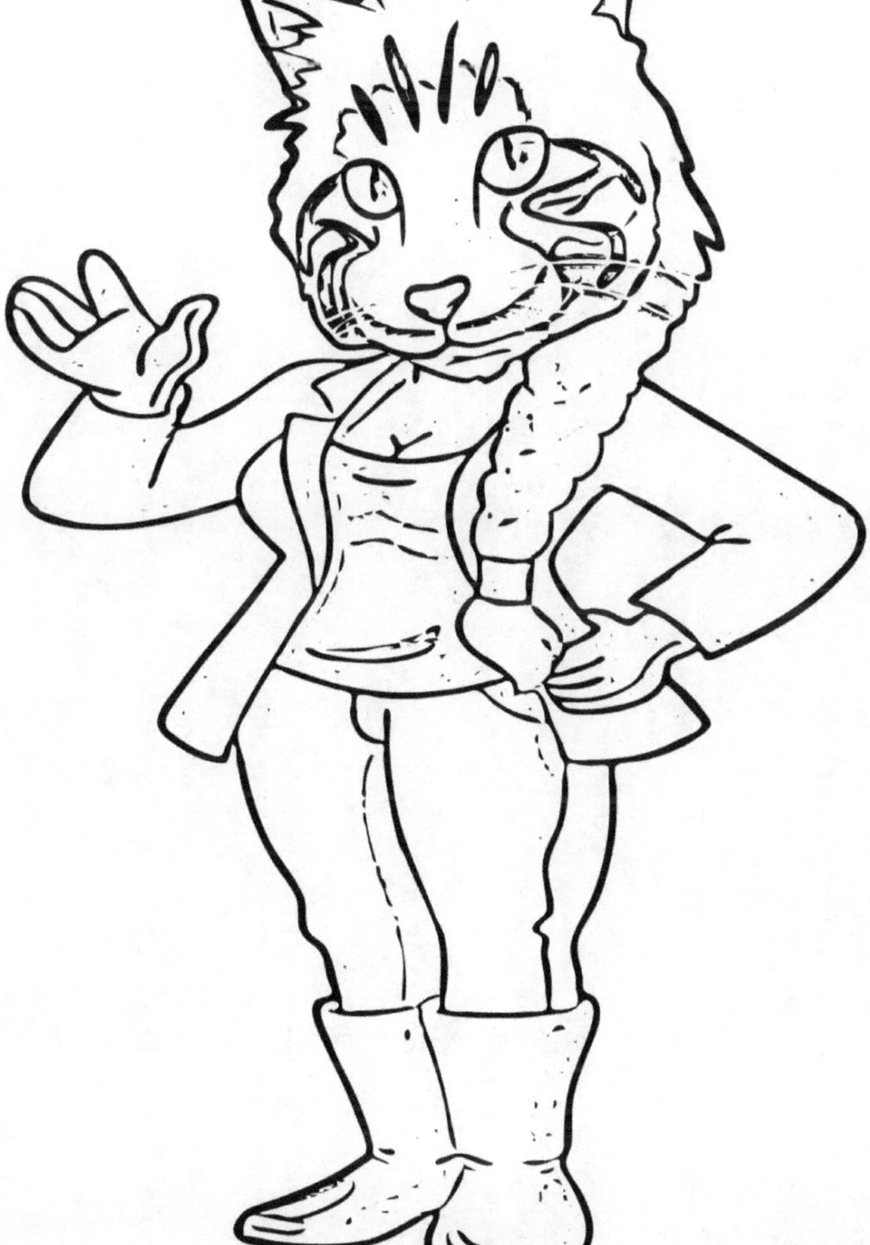

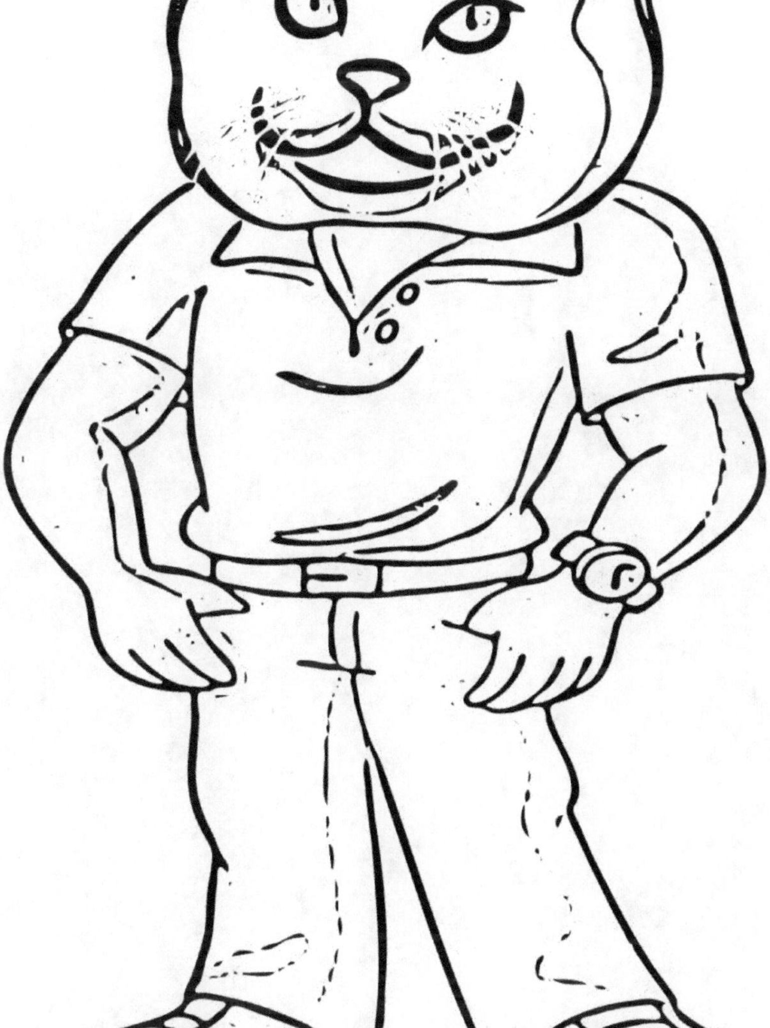

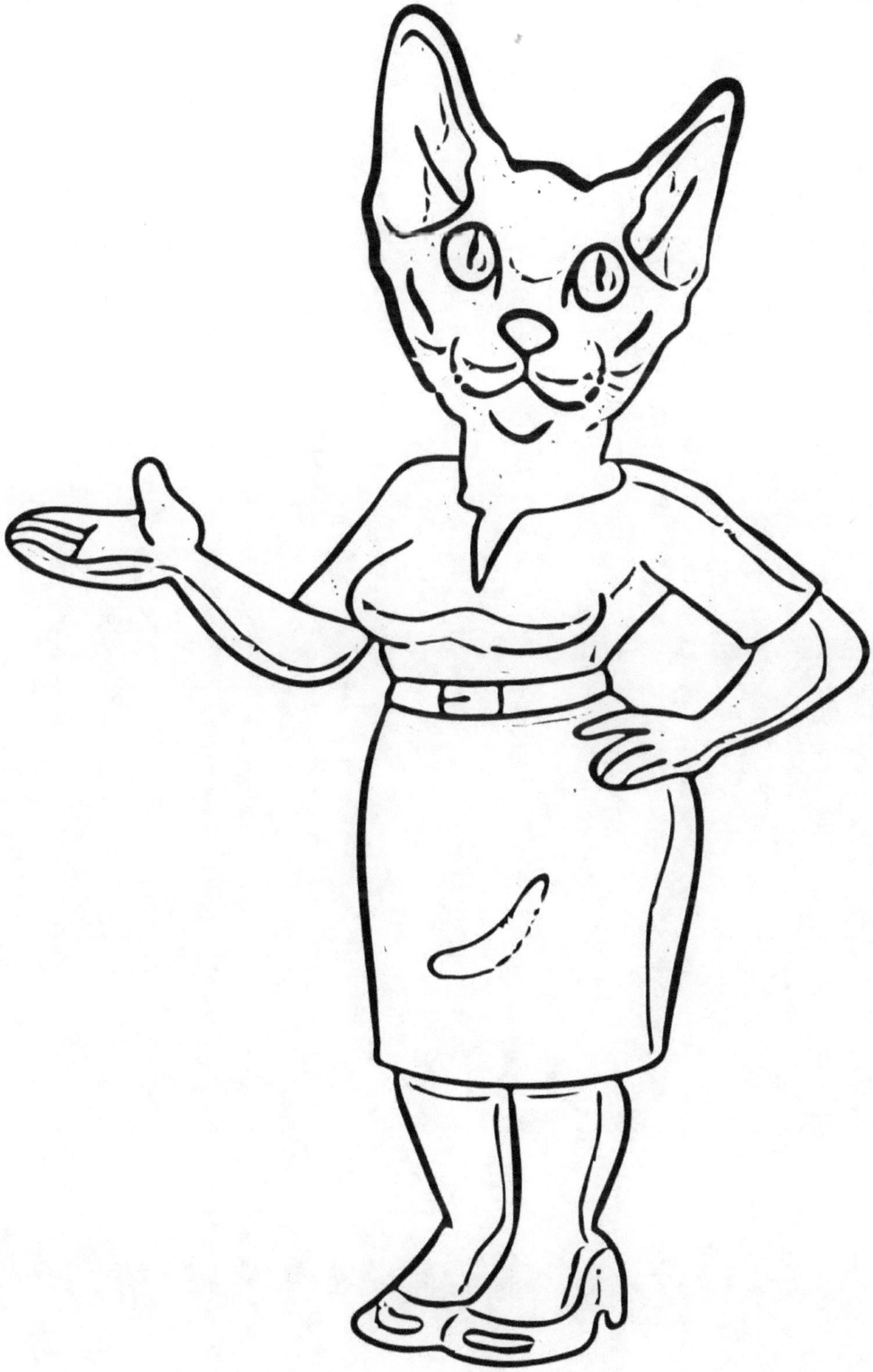

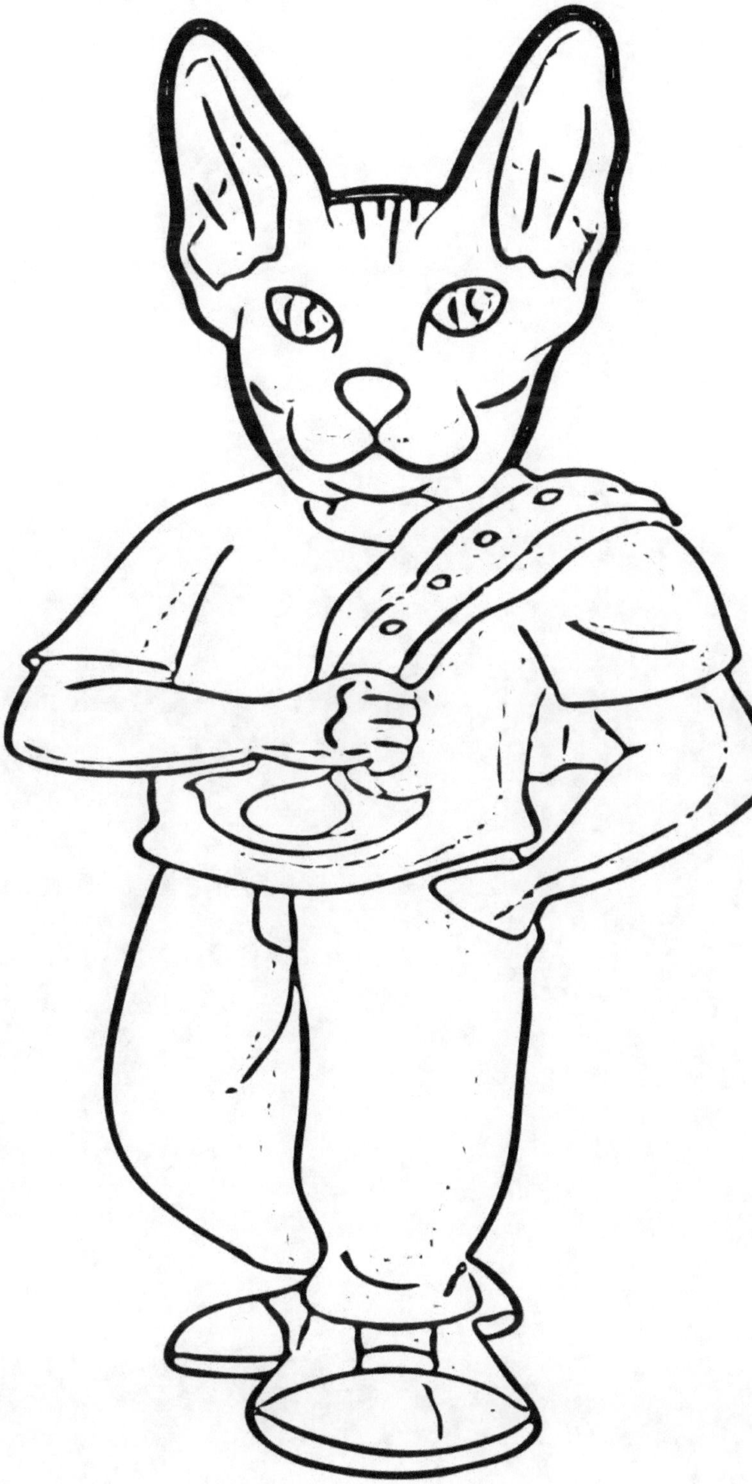

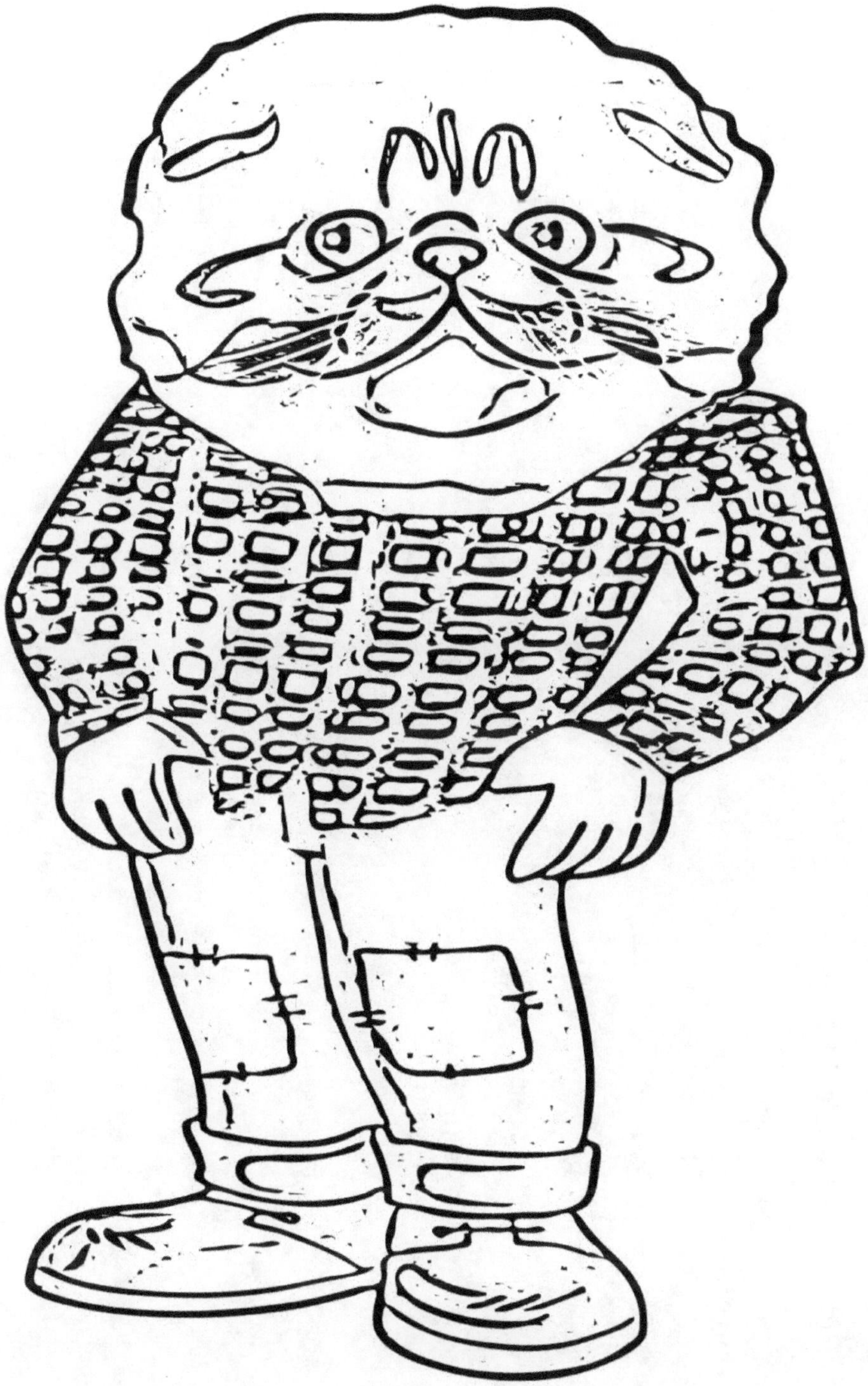

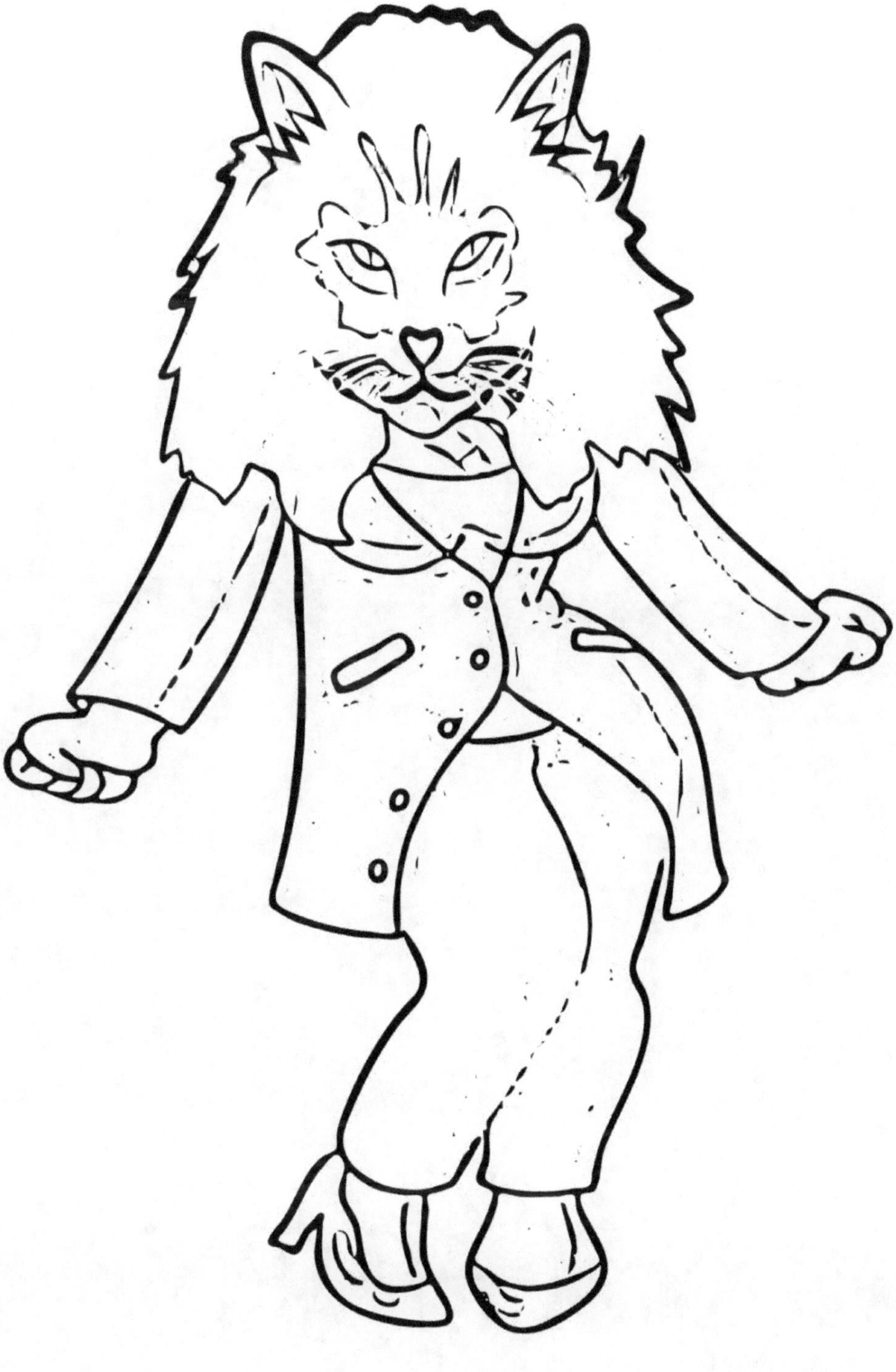

www.ingramcontent.com/pod-product-compliance
Lightning Source LLC
Chambersburg PA
CBHW080610180526
45168CB00007B/2855
* 9 7 8 1 5 1 7 6 0 1 5 9 1 *